THE STORY OF THE BROOKLYN NETS

THE NBA:
A HISTORY
OF HOOPS

THE STORY OF THE
BROOKLYN NETS

NATE FRISCH

CREATIVE EDUCATION

Published by Creative Education
P.O. Box 227, Mankato, Minnesota 56002
Creative Education is an imprint of The Creative Company
www.thecreativecompany.us

Design and production by Blue Design
Art direction by Rita Marshall
Printed in the United States of America

Photographs by Larry Berman, Corbis (Kelly-Mooney
Photography), Getty Images (Nathaniel S. Butler/
NBAE, Lou Capozzola/NBAE, Ned Dishman/NBAE, Sam
Forencich/NBAE, Jesse D. Garrabrant/NBAE, Walter Iooss
Jr./Sports Illustrated, Fernando Medina/NBAE, Manny
Millan/Sports Illustrated, Ronald C. Modra/Sports Imagery,
Layne Murdoch/NBAE, Rich Pilling/NBAE, Dick Raphael/
NBAE, Eliot J. Schechter, Rolf Sjogren, Noren Trotman
/NBAE, Ron Turenne/NBAE), Newscom (Natan Dvir/
Polaris, TANNEN MAURY/EPA, Wang Lei Xinhua News
Agency), Wikipedia (Jim.henderson)

Library of Congress Cataloging-in-Publication Data
Frisch, Nate.
The Story of the Brooklyn Nets / Nate Frisch.
p. cm. — (The NBA: a history of hoops)
Includes index.
Summary: An informative narration of the Brooklyn
Nets professional basketball team's history from its
1967 founding as the New Jersey Americans to today,
spotlighting memorable players and events.
ISBN 978-1-60818-439-2
1. Brooklyn Nets (Basketball team)—History—Juvenile
literature. I. Title.

GV885.52.B76F75 2014
796.323'640974723—dc23   2013037442

CCSS: RI.5.1, 2, 3, 8; RH.6-8.4, 5, 7

First Edition
9 8 7 6 5 4 3 2 1

Cover: Guard Deron Williams
Page 2: Guard Courtney Lee (#6)
Pages 4–5: Forward Julius Erving (#32)
Page 6: Center Brook Lopez

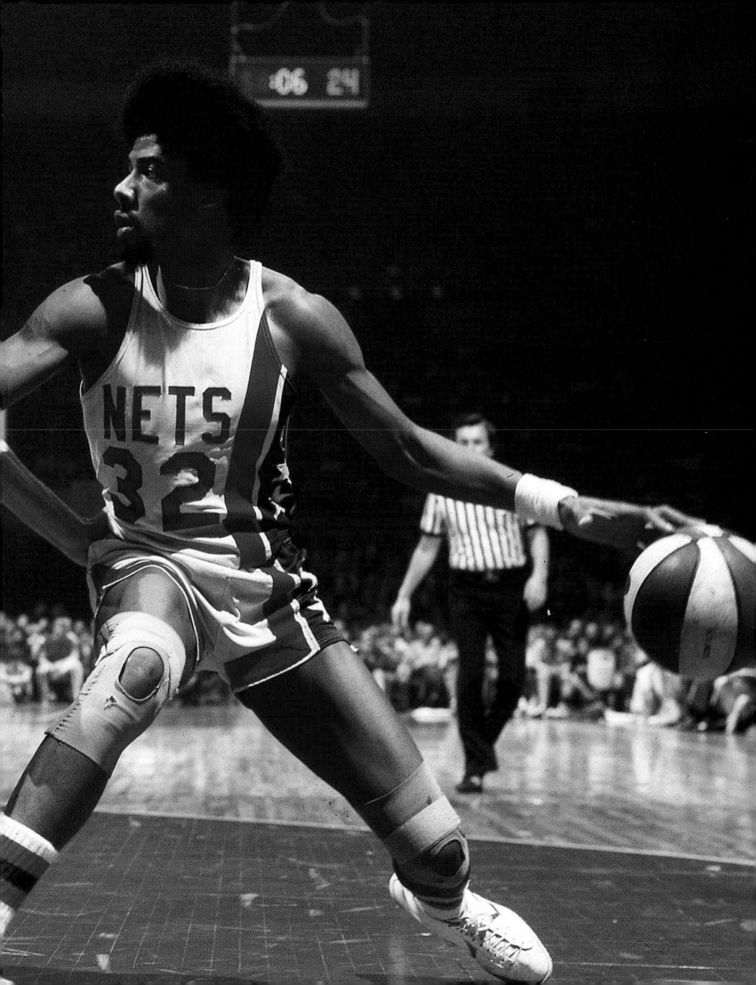

TABLE OF CONTENTS

THE NOMADIC NETS 8

A PRESCRIPTION FOR SUCCESS 16

GLIMPSES OF HOPE 22

BACK TO BASICS 30

A FRANCHISE FACELIFT 40

INDEX 48

COURTSIDE STORIES

HOME-COURT DISADVANTAGE 11

TRUST THE DOCTOR 21

A PLAYOFF SHOCKER 24

THE "SWAMP DRAGONS"? 26

CROSSING THE RIVER AGAIN 39

A TRAGIC NEW BEGINNING 46

INTRODUCING...

BILL MELCHIONNI 13

BUCK WILLIAMS 15

DRAZEN PETROVIC 19

DERRICK COLEMAN 29

JASON KIDD 35

DERON WILLIAMS 43

THE NOMADIC NETS

THE HUDSON RIVER SEPARATES NEW JERSEY FROM THE BUSTLING CITY OF NEW YORK.

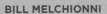

The city of New York, New York, comprises five boroughs, the most populous of which is Brooklyn. First established by Dutch immigrants in 1634 as "Breukelen," it became a focal point of colonial America. After the British took over the settlement in the 1660s, the name changed to Brooklyn. A century later, it was a close witness to the largest battle of the American Revolution as the United States fought to become an independent nation. Ever since, Brooklyn has remained a home to many coexisting immigrants and ethnic groups, embodying the motto "Unity makes strength."

Brooklyn has long appreciated sports. Organized baseball leagues were in place by the mid-1800s, and locals cheered for the Brooklyn Dodgers of Major League Baseball (MLB) starting in 1890. But when the Dodgers

AFTER MANY MOVES, THE NETS FOUND A LONG-TERM HOME IN JERSEY'S MEADOWLANDS.

moved to California before the 1958 season, they left a void until 2012, when a National Basketball Association (NBA) franchise arrived. The incoming club already had a nomadic history of relocations around New York and New Jersey. It was during a previous stop in New York that the club had taken the name "Nets" because it rhymed with Mets and Jets—New York baseball and football teams.

The team that would become the Brooklyn Nets had a shaky beginning. As one of the original members of the American Basketball Association (ABA) in 1967, the club was initially called the Americans. ABA officials wanted the franchise to play in New York City to compete with the NBA's Knicks. But when plans for a home arena in New York fell through, owner Arthur Brown and the Americans settled for Teaneck Armory in New Jersey. The Armory was dim and leaky, and one home game was even postponed because of rain. Fortunately, the team's play was more respectable than its arena.

HOME-COURT DISADVANTAGE

Playing in the Teaneck Armory was often an adventure for the New Jersey Americans in their first season in the ABA. Still, the team achieved a respectable 36–42 record, tied with the Kentucky Colonels for fourth place in the Eastern Division. The two clubs were scheduled to face off in New Jersey in a one-game tiebreaker, with the winner earning a playoff berth. However, a circus was booked at the Armory for the selected date, so the Americans had to look for a new "home" court. The only place management could find on short notice was the aging Commack (or Long Island) Arena on New York's Long Island. When the two clubs and their fans arrived for the game, they discovered that the arena's floor was missing several boards, and the stands were falling apart. ABA commissioner George Mikan ruled the game a forfeit, and New Jersey was eliminated from the playoffs without taking a single shot. Ironically, the Americans moved the next season to a newly repaired Commack Arena, but their bad luck in the building continued, as they finished with a league-low 17–61 record.

Swingman Tony Jackson and guard Levern Tart each averaged at least 19 points per contest, and the New Jersey Americans finished their first season 36–42.

Brown eagerly relocated the team to New York's Long Island the following year, and he believed that the new title "New York Nets" would resonate with local fans. He was wrong. Only an average of 1,108 people showed up to see most of the club's home games. The players also seemed uninterested, ranking last in the ABA in scoring and finishing 17–61. In 1969, a wealthy businessman named Roy Boe bought the team and moved it to a third arena located a little closer to New York City.

Before the 1970–71 season, Boe hired popular local college coach Lou Carnesecca to take over the reins of the club and engineered a trade for the team's first superstar, forward Rick Barry. Barry had been one of the top scorers in the NBA but jumped leagues because of a contract dispute with his former club, the San Francisco Warriors. "Rick was a scoring machine," said Kentucky Colonels forward Dan Issel, a future

Basketball Hall-of-Famer. "I once heard him say that he expected to score 30 points a night. He had it all figured out: he'd take 20 shots, make 12, and then he'd get to the foul line 6 or 8 times to pick up the rest. He talked about it like anyone could do it."

Barry, point guard Bill Melchionni, and center Billy "The Whopper" Paultz helped the Nets post a winning record for the first time in 1971–72. The club even reached the final round of the ABA playoffs that year before losing the championship to the Indiana Pacers.

BILL MELCHIONNI

POSITION GUARD
HEIGHT 6-FOOT-1
NETS SEASONS
1969–76

As an All-American guard at Villanova University, Bill Melchionni ranked ninth in the nation in scoring. Then he was drafted by the powerful Philadelphia 76ers, who were led by center Wilt Chamberlain, and he learned to pass first and shoot second. He carried this valuable lesson with him when he switched leagues and joined the Nets in 1969. Melchionni quickly became the glue that held the Nets' offense together. In his first year in New York, Melchionni averaged 15.2 points and 5.7 assists a game. He blossomed the next season, 1970–71, leading the ABA in assists (with a total of 672) while also averaging 17.6 points per game. Melchionni topped the league in assists the next year as well and was also the point man in the Nets' devastating press defense. He helped the Nets win ABA championships in 1974 as a player and in 1976 as a player/assistant coach. The 1976 ABA title game was Melchionni's last as a player, but his retired number 25 Nets jersey soon hung proudly from the rafters in the Izod Center at the Meadowlands.

BUCK WILLIAMS

When the Nets selected Buck Williams out of the University of Maryland with the third pick in the 1981 NBA Draft, they knew they were getting a hard-nosed competitor and an outstanding person. Williams spent the first 8 of his 17 NBA seasons in New Jersey and set most of the team's career scoring and rebounding records. As of 2014, he was 1 of only 12 NBA players to have amassed 16,000 points and 13,000 rebounds. At 6-foot-8 and 215 pounds, Williams wasn't the biggest man on the court, but he was one of the strongest. He knew how to establish a dominant rebounding position and also played outstanding defense. Williams earned respect not only for his playing ability but also for his sportsmanship. "I think players have an obligation to the public to carry themselves in a certain way," Williams once said. "I never wanted to do anything to embarrass myself, the organization, or my family. My father always told me that a good name means more than a million dollars." The Nets retired his number 52 jersey in 1999.

A PRESCRIPTION FOR SUCCESS

DOUBLE-TEAMING COULDN'T CONTAIN GUARD OTIS BIRDSONG'S TENACIOUS OFFENSE.

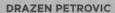

T he team's prospects suffered a serious blow before the next season when a judge ruled that Barry had to return to the Warriors to complete his contract. Boe soon made up for the loss by trading with the Virginia Squires for highflying Julius Erving, who was nicknamed "Dr. J" for the way he "operated" on the court. The 6-foot-6 forward moved with astonishing speed and grace, and his soaring dunks filled sports highlight films. "Doc goes up and never comes down," said Melchionni.

The Nets didn't come down, either, during the 1973–74 season, Dr. J's first with the club. They won 55 regular-season games, a 25-game improvement. Then the Nets routed the Utah Stars in the league finals to win their first ABA championship, and Dr. J earned his own title— ABA Most Valuable Player (MVP). Two seasons later,

DRAZEN PETROVIC

POSITION GUARD
HEIGHT 6-FOOT-5
NETS SEASONS
1990–93

Perhaps the best words to describe Drazen Petrovic were "high energy." Chuck Daly, who coached Petrovic in his final Nets season, called him "indefatigable" because he never seemed to get tired. He was a whirlwind on the court and one of the best long-range shooters in NBA history. Petrovic grew up in a small city in Croatia near the Adriatic Sea. There he practiced for hours every day before and after school, putting up as many as 1,000 shots from all over the court. At age 15, he was named to the Yugoslavian national team and four years later was playing professionally in Spain. By age 25, he was in America as a member of the Portland Trail Blazers and then joined the Nets during the 1990–91 season. "Petro" quickly established himself as one of the league's top three-point shooters. A true pioneer, Petrovic's success in the NBA laid the groundwork for other European stars to come and play in the U.S. Almost a decade after his tragic death in 1993, Petrovic was elected to the Basketball Hall of Fame in 2002.

the Nets staged a virtual replay of their first championship campaign. They duplicated their 55–29 record, Dr. J again led the league in scoring with an average of 29.3 points per game, and New York romped to its second—and last—ABA title.

The 1975–76 season marked the end of the ABA's brief history, for in the summer of 1976, the ABA and NBA merged, with the Nets and three other ABA franchises joining the older league. But becoming an NBA franchise cost the Nets dearly. The team was required to pay a $3-million entry fee to the NBA and an additional $4.8 million to the Knicks to be allowed to share their region. The financial fallout made it impossible for Dr. J to receive a promised raise, forcing Boe to sell Erving's contract to the Philadelphia 76ers even before Dr. J could play his first NBA game with the Nets. "How could anyone do this to us?" wondered New York guard "Super John" Williamson. "Our season is over already." Williamson turned out to be right. Without the Doctor, the 1976–77 Nets could not be saved from a dismal 22–60 record.

Before the next season, Boe moved the Nets back to their original state, and the New Jersey Nets were officially born in September 1977. The team also acquired a new offensive star—sensational rookie forward Bernard King. During the Nets' first years in New Jersey, the nucleus of King, Williamson, and shot-blocking center George Johnson kept the Nets near the middle of the NBA standings, but the team continued to post losing records. By the 1979–80 season,

King and Williamson were traded away as Nets management searched for a winning combination of talent.

Things began to come together in New Jersey two years later when veteran NBA coach Larry Brown took over the team. Brown's first move was to select 21-year-old power forward Buck Williams in the 1981 NBA Draft. A rugged rebounder and scorer, Williams averaged 12.3 boards and 15.5 points per game to win the NBA Rookie of the Year award. "Every team should be blessed with a Buck Williams," said former Nets star Rick Barry. "He's consistent, hardworking, and tough."

Coach Brown combined Williams with guards Micheal Ray Richardson and Otis Birdsong, "dunk-meister" Darryl Dawkins at center, and sharpshooting forward Albert King (Bernard's younger brother) to create a well-balanced unit in 1982-83. Playing for the second season in the Brendan Byrne Arena (later named the Izod Center) in the Meadowlands sports complex of northern New Jersey, the Nets earned the third-best record in the Eastern Conference's Atlantic Division. Everything was looking up until the last two weeks of the season, when Brown announced that he would be leaving the team to coach at the University of Kansas. Brown's decision seemed to deflate the young Nets, who quickly shuffled out of the playoffs.

The team stayed above .500 for two more seasons under new coach Stan Albeck and even pulled off a major upset by eliminating Julius Erving's 76ers in an exciting first-round matchup in the 1984 playoffs. Then the Nets went on an extended drought for the rest of the 1980s, reaching their low point when they assembled a franchise-worst 17–65 record in 1989–90.

TRUST THE DOCTOR

During the Nets' run to their first ABA championship in 1974, they faced off against the Kentucky Colonels in the second round of the playoffs. The Colonels, led by center Artis Gilmore and forward Dan Issel, always gave the Nets problems. Still, New York won the first two games of the series at home. Game 3 came down to the final seconds tied 87–87, and Nets coach Kevin Loughery called timeout to set up a last play. Forward Julius Erving laid a hand on the coach's shoulder and said, "Kevin, I'll take the last shot." Loughery nodded and then said, "Okay, guys, but if Doc misses—" Erving cut off the coach again, saying, "Kevin, I won't miss." Erving received the inbounds pass, waited a few seconds to let the clock run down, and then drove towards his right. He leaped off the wrong foot and banked the shot in from an almost impossible angle for the win. Everyone in the arena was stunned. The Nets completed the series sweep three nights later and then easily captured the ABA Finals for their first league title.

GLIMPSES
OF HOPE

KENNY ANDERSON'S LACKLUSTER ROOKIE SEASON DIDN'T REFLECT THE FUTURE ALL-STAR'S TALENTS.

During the Nets' down years, team management committed several blunders in the NBA Draft. First-round picks such as guard Dwayne "Pearl" Washington and forward Chris Morris, who were stars in college, turned out to be busts in the pros. Then, under new coach Bill Fitch, the club made two outstanding draft picks in the early 1990s—power forward Derrick Coleman and point guard Kenny Anderson. Talented but moody, Coleman could dominate games when he was motivated, hitting 18-foot jumpers with deadly accuracy or making daring moves inside. Anderson was an outstanding passer and penetrator, but, like Coleman, he could be inconsistent.

This talented duo, along with long-range bomber Drazen Petrovic from Croatia—the NBA's first European star—powered the Nets to a 43–39 record in 1992–93, ending a

A PLAYOFF SHOCKER

Before the 1984 playoffs, the Nets had qualified for the NBA postseason three times but had yet to win a single playoff game. Their chances didn't look good in 1984, either, as they would be facing the defending NBA champion Philadelphia 76ers, led by former Nets star Julius Erving. New Jersey shocked the 76ers and most basketball experts by taking the first two games of the series in Philadelphia. Then they headed home looking for a series sweep. But Erving and guard Maurice Cheeks took over, leading Philly to consecutive wins in the Meadowlands and setting up a deciding Game 5 showdown in Philadelphia. Erving assured reporters that the Nets would not win a third time in Philadelphia. "You can mail in the stats," he proclaimed. Erving's prediction looked solid as Philly took a seven-point lead into the closing minutes of the contest. Then guard Micheal Ray Richardson and forward Albert King led a Nets charge that resulted in a thrilling 101–98 victory. The Nets franchise would suffer through the rest of the 1980s, but for one night, the team was a big winner.

seven-year streak of losing seasons. Then, in the summer of 1993, Petrovic was tragically killed in a car accident in Europe when he was there for an off-season tournament. Basketball fans on both sides of the Atlantic Ocean mourned his death. "It's hard for you to imagine here in America, because you have so many great players," Drazen's brother, Aleksander, said. "But we are a country of 4 million. Without him, basketball [in Croatia] takes three steps back."

Without Petrovic, the Nets and their fans experienced a bittersweet season in 1993–94. The club achieved its second straight winning record (45–37), and both Coleman and Anderson were selected to play in the All-Star Game. But New Jersey was quickly eliminated in the first round of the playoffs by the rival Knicks. Beset by injuries the next year, the Nets fell below .500 again, and team management decided to clean house. Coleman and Anderson

MICHEAL RAY RICHARDSON AVERAGED 16.1 POINTS AND 6.8 ASSISTS PER GAME FOR THE NETS.

THE "SWAMP DRAGONS"?

Despite the team's improvement in the early 1990s, the Nets still had trouble attracting fans to their arena in the Meadowlands. In contrast, the New Jersey Devils hockey team usually played to packed houses in the same arena. So Nets management decided that their club needed a new, livelier image. One marketing executive suggested that a name as catchy as "Devils" might excite fans. He proposed calling the team the "New Jersey Swamp Dragons." The name had a double meaning. Since the site of the Meadowlands had originally been a swamp, it would be historically fitting. More important for marketing purposes, though, was that swamp dragons were lovable pets in a series of popular graphic novels called Discworld. The marketing executive envisioned a colorful new logo, based on the graphic novel illustrations, which might excite young fans and prompt them to buy more team merchandise. The team proposed the new name to the NBA's executive committee, where it was rejected by a close vote. The club explored a few other names but decided to stick with "Nets" in the end.

"IT'S HARD FOR YOU TO IMAGINE HERE IN AMERICA, BECAUSE YOU HAVE SO MANY GREAT PLAYERS, BUT WE ARE A COUNTRY OF 4 MILLION. WITHOUT HIM, BASKETBALL [IN CROATIA] TAKES THREE STEPS BACK."

— ALEKSANDER PETROVIC ON HIS BROTHER, DRAZEN

were traded during the 1995–96 season, and more deals followed. New arrivals included guard Kendall Gill and 7-foot-6 center Shawn Bradley. Nets fans needed a scorecard to figure out just who was on the floor for their team.

The wheeling and dealing continued into the 1997 NBA Draft when New Jersey sent several players and its first-round pick to Philadelphia for the rights to All-American forward Keith Van Horn, the second pick in the Draft. Long and lean, Van Horn was a small forward in a power forward's body. "North to south, up and down the court, he's the fastest big man in the country," said Utah Jazz president Frank Layden. Along with his speed, Van Horn displayed intensity on the boards and possessed an excellent outside shot. He combined with second-year guard Kerry Kittles and power forward Jayson Williams to key an explosive offense that led the Nets back to the playoffs.

The team's revival was short-lived, however, and New Jersey sank quickly to the bottom of the Atlantic Division for the next three years. In an effort to turn things around during the 1998–99 season, the Nets pulled off a blockbuster midseason trade with the Minnesota Timberwolves, obtaining high-scoring point guard Stephon Marbury. Marbury's presence greatly improved the team's offense, but he hindered the club's defense when he collided with Williams, the club's best shot-blocker and rebounder, under the New Jersey basket in a late-season contest. Williams suffered a severely broken leg that ended his career.

DERRICK COLEMAN

POSITION FORWARD
HEIGHT 6-FOOT-10
NETS SEASONS
1990–95

Derrick Coleman had the body and skills to be an NBA great. But it seemed he never wanted to work hard enough to become a real star. A first-team All-American out of Syracuse University, Coleman was the first overall pick in the 1990 NBA Draft. The Nets obtained a forceful rebounder with a soft touch from the outside who was also an excellent passer for a big man. During his 5 seasons in New Jersey, "D.C." averaged 19.9 points, 10.6 rebounds, and 3.1 assists per game. Such numbers were good enough to earn him NBA Rookie of the Year honors in 1991 and selection as a league All-Star in 1994. But New Jersey coaches also had to deal with Coleman's poor attitude and occasional laziness, and a contract dispute led the Nets to trade him after the 1994–95 season. While Coleman didn't live up to his basketball potential, he did achieve several other lifetime goals. Following retirement, he used his basketball earnings to build a strip mall in his hometown of Detroit, Michigan, and helped revitalize the neighborhood in which he had grown up.

BACK TO BASICS

FORWARD RICHARD JEFFERSON HELPED THE NETS BECOME A POSTSEASON FORCE.

s the new century began, the Nets reached back to their ABA days to hire Rod Thorn as team president. Thorn had been a Nets assistant coach when the team won its first ABA championship in 1974. He had later earned a reputation as an astute basketball executive for his role in drafting star guard Michael Jordan. Thorn was now determined to build a strong foundation in New Jersey. His first move was to select forward Kenyon Martin with the top overall pick in the 2000 NBA Draft. Martin loved to battle around the basket for rebounds and emphasized defense before offense. To prove the point, Martin chose six as his uniform number in honor of Bill Russell, one of the best defenders in NBA history.

Thorn's next moves truly turned things around in New Jersey. He hired former Los Angeles Lakers guard Byron

KENYON MARTIN'S SCRAPPY DEFENSE CREATED KEY SCORING OPPORTUNITIES FOR THE NETS.

Scott to coach the Nets and made a draft-day trade in 2001 to bring in rookie small forward Richard Jefferson, whose slashing drives to the basket provided a new dimension to the team's offense. Thorn then engineered a high-level trade of All-Stars with the Phoenix Suns in July 2001, sending Marbury out west in exchange for point guard Jason Kidd, one of the NBA's all-time greatest passers. Kidd was more than just an outstanding individual player; his presence improved the whole team. Danny Ainge, a basketball analyst who had once coached Kidd, described his impact on the Nets. "This team has taken on Jason's soul," said Ainge. "Some guys show up to play; some guys show up to win. But the way Jason plays, he elevates everyone else's game because they go, 'My gosh, look at how hard he plays, look how confident he is, look at how tough-minded he is.' It's contagious for the rest of them. They see how hard you have to play to win."

Following Kidd's lead, New Jersey pulled off a 26-game turnaround, going 52–30 and, incredibly, making it all the way to the 2002 NBA Finals. There, the team's championship dreams were quickly crushed by the powerful Lakers, led by center Shaquille O'Neal and guard Kobe Bryant. However, the Nets landed on their feet the following season, topping the Atlantic Division once more and winning 12 of their first 14 playoff games to reach the NBA Finals again. This time, they faced off against the San Antonio Spurs and star center/forward Tim Duncan. The clubs split the first four games, and then San Antonio swept the final two contests to claim the championship.

With two straight Finals appearances under their belt, the Nets and their fans were confident that an NBA title would soon be in their grasp. Then a rift between Kidd and Coach Scott led Thorn to fire Scott during the next season and replace him with assistant coach Lawrence Frank. Frank's high-energy style helped to revitalize the squad, and the Nets won 14 straight games on the way to their third consecutive Atlantic Division title.

JASON KIDD

POSITION GUARD, COACH
HEIGHT 6-FOOT-4
NETS SEASONS
AS PLAYER 2001–08, AS
COACH 2013-PRESENT

For New Jersey Nets fans, July 18, 2001, was one of the most significant days in team history. That's when Jason Kidd was traded to the Nets from the Phoenix Suns. Kidd had only average straight-line speed and a below-average outside shot, but he possessed the skills and leadership needed to rally a group of individual players into a winning team. Nets coach Byron Scott was thrilled to have Kidd join his club. "He's a one-man fast break who's quicker with the ball than most NBA players are without it, plus he's a devastating on-the-ball defender and an excellent rebounder," said Scott. "He pushes the ball up, gets us into the open floor, and creates easy shot after easy shot. That's what winning basketball is all about at this level." The unselfish point guard lifted a struggling Nets franchise out of the gutter, and it reached the postseason during each of Kidd's six full years in New Jersey. A 10-time All-Star, Kidd retired in 2013 but returned to his beloved Nets as their head coach.

It was clear that some of the team's magic was beginning to fade, though, when New Jersey was eliminated in just the second round of the playoffs.

Roster turmoil and injuries to key team members plagued the Nets in 2004–05. Martin and Kittles left town via trades. Then both Kidd and Jefferson spent part of the year on injured reserve. The team seemed doomed until New Jersey traded with the Toronto Raptors for skywalking swingman Vince Carter. Carter's athletic dunks and long-range shooting thrilled New Jersey fans. He gave the club an amazing new offensive weapon, and once Kidd and Jefferson returned to the lineup, the Nets were ready to soar. The club won 16 of its last 21 games to slip into the playoffs with a 42–40 record, only to be swept in the first round by the Miami Heat.

LAWRENCE FRANK'S ATTENTION TO DETAIL HELPED THE NETS REACH THE PLAYOFFS FOUR TIMES.

VINCE CARTER'S FAMOUS
VERTICAL LEAPS HELPED
HIM SHATTER FRANCHISE
SCORING RECORDS.

37

CROSSING THE RIVER AGAIN

In August 2004, an investor group led by businessman Bruce Ratner purchased the Nets. Other owners included hip-hop musician Jay-Z and mystery novelist Mary Higgins Clark. Soon afterwards, Ratner announced his intention to move the club back across the Hudson River and into a proposed new arena to be built in Brooklyn, believing the Nets could fare much better financially in New York than in New Jersey. Some of the Nets' oldest fans, those who had cheered the club in its ABA days as the New York Nets, were thrilled that the team might be moving close to them again. Yet Ratner's plans were stalled by problems in obtaining funding for the new arena or getting permission to build it on land that had been promised by New York City for other purposes. To save money, Ratner prompted management to trade several of the team's highest-priced players—such as guard Kerry Kittles and forward Kenyon Martin—for players with less expensive or shorter-term contracts. A few years later in 2012, the new-look Nets finally made the trip over the river to their new Brooklyn home at Barclays Center.

A FRANCHISE FACELIFT

SOFT-SPOKEN GUARD DEVIN HARRIS LET HIS OFFENSIVE GAME SPEAK FOR ITSELF.

wnership of the Nets franchise had changed hands in 2004, and in 2005, the new owners expressed plans to relocate to Brooklyn. Not surprisingly, this was a tough pill for New Jersey fans to swallow. But since Brooklyn didn't even have an arena yet, the Nets would have to spend several more years trying to impress jaded fans in "The Garden State."

On the court, the club tried to soothe hard feelings with entertaining play. After a mediocre start in 2005–06, the Nets went on a 14-game winning tear, sparked by the talented perimeter of Kidd, Jefferson, and Carter. The late surge earned the club its fourth division title in five years. New Jersey bested the Pacers in the opening round before again colliding with Miami. The Heat, led by guard Dwyane Wade and center Shaquille O'Neal, scorched the Nets on

their way to an NBA championship.

The 2006–07 season was more of the same, but this time, a loss in the second round of the playoffs came at the hands of forward LeBron James and the Cleveland Cavaliers. Then, when the Nets appeared to be out of playoff contention in 2007–08, Kidd requested a trade to a more promising club. The Nets granted Kidd's wish by sending him to the Dallas Mavericks in exchange for guard Devin Harris. Although the organization and fans would miss Kidd, the much younger Harris was a quick ball handler and showed great potential as he finished out the season.

Unfortunately for Harris, he would soon lose his talented wingmen, as the high-priced Jefferson and Carter were dealt away

in successive off-seasons (2008 and 2009 respectively). During that two-season span, the Nets went younger and bigger by drafting seven-footer Brook Lopez in the 2008 Draft and trading for power forward Kris Humphries during the 2009–10 campaign.

The new core roster had potential, but inexperience translated to losses. In 2009–10, Coach Frank was dismissed during the youthful Nets' 18-game losing streak that opened the season. They eventually limped to the finish line with a 12–70 record. "It was an abysmal season," Harris summed up.

Before the 2010–11 season, the Nets brought in head coach Avery Johnson from Dallas. New Jersey's young frontcourt showed improvement, as Lopez averaged 20.4 points per game, and

DERON WILLIAMS

POSITION GUARD
HEIGHT 6-FOOT-3
NETS SEASONS
2010–PRESENT

When the Nets acquired point guard Deron Williams in a trade with the Utah Jazz during the 2010–11 season, they were taking a risk on a double-edged sword. Williams had earned a reputation as a headstrong floor general who challenged even his own coaches about how to run an offense. On the other hand, no one could question Williams's ability to create easy shots for teammates while also being a daring scorer himself. The fiery point guard also made the Nets an alluring option to other NBA stars who wanted to team up with the competitive and unselfish leader. Yet for all the stories of his intense nature, Williams had fun in the NBA. During a strong start to the 2012–13 season, he sat, in full uniform, among the media at the press conference of his straight-laced coach, Avery Johnson. When his turn came up, Williams inquired, "I think what everyone wants to know is, who is the best team in New York?" Johnson responded, "It's not about having the best team in New York. My point guard talks about being the best team in the NBA, and that's what I want for him."

A TRAGIC NEW BEGINNING

When the Brooklyn Nets moved into the brand-new Barclays Center in 2012, the last thing they expected was that soggy weather would postpone games as it had during the franchise's first season. But as the Nets prepared for a highly anticipated home opener against the New York Knicks, a storm was brewing. Hurricane Sandy had begun in the Caribbean and was heading north along the East Coast. "I think the guys have got more butterflies about Sandy," coach Avery Johnson said in response to the team's nerves about the opener. "Once that passes, I'm sure obviously the game is on their mind." The storm did not pass. Instead, its high winds and tons of water devastated New York City, claiming lives and causing billions of dollars' worth in damages. Although Barclays Center held up, subways were flooded and power was knocked out in much of the city. The game was postponed. "We're definitely disappointed,… but we realize the seriousness of the situation," commented Nets guard Deron Williams. "A lot of people have lost homes and lost loved ones, so in the grand scheme of things, [the game is] not really that important."

Humphries pulled down 10.4 boards per contest. Even so, the club's record was embarrassing by late February. It was then that the Nets swung a blockbuster trade, giving up multiple players (including Harris) and draft selections to bring in point guard Deron Williams. Williams had averaged better than 18 points and 10 assists per game in each of the previous 3 seasons with the Jazz. "He is one of the premier point guards in the NBA," said Nets general manager Billy King. "And his skill and talent level will bolster our franchise as we continue to build toward our goal of becoming a championship-caliber team."

illiams didn't conjure up miracles overnight. The 2010-11 campaign was beyond saving, and clouds loomed over the next season as well. The 2011–12 season would be the team's last in New Jersey, and keeping fans interested was a challenge. Williams was under contract for only one season, and a nervous front office held off on any other roster upgrades until they knew if he'd return. The Nets just seemed to kill time on their way to a 22–44 finish.

The sky cleared in 2012–13. The club moved to its new home of Barclays Center in Brooklyn, Williams extended his contract, and smooth shooting guard Joe Johnson arrived. Also starting his first full year with the Nets was multitalented forward Gerald Wallace. The revamped roster took the court in retro-styled black-and-white uniforms, breaking away from the red, white, and blue color scheme that dated back to the New Jersey Americans.

After a strong start to the 2012–13 season, the Nets started to skid, prompting management to replace Coach Johnson with assistant coach P. J. Carlesimo. The change seemed to help, and Brooklyn earned the fourth-best record in the Eastern Conference. Unfortunately, a gritty Bulls team edged out the Nets in a first-round upset. Nonetheless, players remained confident that, moving forward, they would work out the kinks. "I think this experience is going to make us tougher as a group," Williams said. "We can be good, and we've shown glimpses of being a really good team."

The Nets took team-building to the next level during the summer of 2013, hiring former All-Star Jason Kidd as head coach and trading for Boston Celtics veterans Kevin Garnett and Paul Pierce. Although the team and its new coach started the season just 10–21, the Nets' fortunes turned around when their expensive cast of stars finally began clicking in January. "We were a different team, our mind-set was different, and the way we played was different," said guard Shaun Livingston. Even after Lopez suffered a season-ending foot injury, Brooklyn recorded its longest home winning streak in team history and rolled into the playoffs, where it was eliminated by Miami in the conference semifinals.

Like the borough of Brooklyn, the Nets have become stronger by presenting a unified front. Regardless of the state in which they have played, the Nets have frequently demonstrated the power of teamwork and the benefits of diversity. As the wandering Nets settle into their 7th home, and as Brooklyn welcomes its first major sports franchise in 55 years, hopes are high that the connection will bring the franchise and its fans their first NBA title.

INDEX

ABA championships 13, 17, 20, 21, 31
ABA Finals 12, 21
ABA-NBA merger 20
ABA seasons 10, 11, 12, 13, 20, 21, 31, 39
Albeck, Stan 20
All-Star Game 25
Anderson, Kenny 23, 25
Barclays Center 39, 46, 47
Barry, Rick 12, 17, 20
Basketball Hall of Fame 19
Birdsong, Otis 20
Boe, Roy 12, 17, 20
Bradley, Shawn 28
Brendan Byrne Arena 20
Brown, Arthur 10, 12
Brown, Larry 20
Carlesimo, P. J. 47
Carnesecca, Lou 12
Carter, Vince 36, 41, 42
Coleman, Derrick 23, 25, 29
Commack Arena 11
Dawkins, Darryl 20
division championships 34, 41
Erving, Julius 17, 20, 21, 24
Fitch, Bill 23
Frank, Lawrence 34, 42
Garnett, Kevin 47
Gill, Kendall 28
Harris, Devin 42, 47

Humphries, Kris 42, 47
Izod Center 13, 20
Jackson, Tony 12
Jefferson, Richard 34, 36, 41, 42
Johnson, Avery 42, 43, 46, 47
Johnson, George 20
Johnson, Joe 47
Kidd, Jason 34, 35, 36, 41, 42, 47
King, Albert 20, 24
King, Bernard 20
King, Billy 47
Kittles, Kerry 28, 36, 39
Livingston, Shaun 47
Lopez, Brook 42
Loughery, Kevin 21
Marbury, Stephon 28, 34
Martin, Kenyon 31, 36, 39
Melchionni, Bill 12, 13, 17
Mikan, George 11
Morris, Chris 23
MVP award 17
NBA Finals 34
Paultz, Billy 12
Petrovic, Drazen 19, 23, 25
Pierce, Paul 47
playoffs 11, 12, 20, 21, 24, 25, 28, 34, 35, 36, 41, 42, 47
Ratner, Bruce 39
retired numbers 13, 15
Richardson, Micheal Ray 20, 24
Rookie of the Year award 20, 29

Scott, Byron 31, 34, 35
Tart, Levern 12
team name 10, 12, 26
team records 11, 12, 17, 20, 23, 25, 34, 36, 42, 47
Teaneck Armory 10, 11
Thorn, Rod 31, 34
Van Horn, Keith 28
Wallace, Gerald 47
Washington, Dwayne "Pearl" 23
Williams, Buck 15, 20
Williams, Deron 43, 46, 47
Williams, Jayson 28
Williamson, John 20